BOYISHLY

BOYISHLY TANYA OLSON

YESYES BOOKS PORTLAND

FIRST EDITION, 2013
ISBN 978-1-936919-14-7
PRINTED IN THE UNITED STATES OF AMERICA

PUBLISHED BY YESYES BOOKS
1232 NE PRESCOTT STREET
PORTLAND, OR 97211
YESYESBOOKS.COM

KMA SULLIVAN, PUBLISHER
JUSTIN BOENING, LEAD EDITOR FOR *BOYISHLY*
STEPHEN DANOS, ASSISTANT EDITOR
HAFIZAH GETER, ASSISTANT EDITOR
JILL KOLONGOWSKI, MANAGING EDITOR
MARK DERKS, FICTION EDITOR, *VINYL POETRY*
PHILIP B. WILLIAMS, POETRY EDITOR, *VINYL POETRY*
ALBAN FISCHER, GRAPHIC DESIGNER
THOMAS PATRICK LEVY, WEBSITE DESIGN AND DEVELOPMENT

For Beth and for Nicholas

He was young; he was boyish;
he did but as nature bade him do.

—**VIRGINIA WOOLF**
Orlando

CONTENTS

III

BOYISHLY

EXCLUDE
ALL
OTHER
THOUGHTS

Begin by knowing what an honor
we undertake together tonight. Treat
everything of this evening as an honor.
Rinse your hands to the wrists, backs first,
as an honor. Palm water over your eyes,
to your mouth, as an honor. Pay honor
to the corpse face up atop the table.
Sit to the right of the body, in honor.
Know what is about to begin
exists only as honor.

Stay at the body's side, both hands
upon the corpse, until nightfall.
Until nightfall, think whatever thoughts
present themselves to be thought. Think
of your desires. Think of what you hope
to achieve. Think of who you imagine
you'll be come the morning. Think of this
in daylight, as come night
you must think only of your words.
In the night, only your words
may run through your mind
and they must run on a loop
like the frames of a movie, one word
entering focus, leaving only
when the next pushes it from the light.
Although there is always room

in the mind for other thoughts,
there must be no other thoughts.

At nightfall, with only your words
running through your mind, climb
upon the corpse. Lying atop the corpse,
place your mouth upon its mouth.
Pull its body to your body. Hold it
tightly to you. Think only of your words.
This part of the night may feel like the longest,
for, although it is the calmest, there is nothing
to do but lie mouth to mouth with a corpse,
excluding all other thoughts.

At some point in the night, the corpse
will begin to move. Though the movement
is merely fitful at first—fluttering lids, rolling
eyes, twitching thighs—it is nonetheless
alarming. Continue to hold the corpse
securely to you, your mouth upon its mouth.
The corpse will thrash and buck
trying to free itself; think only
of your words. The corpse will stand
and shudder violently. Its elasticity,
its determination to rid itself of you
is shocking. It is impossible to imagine

the desperation of a corpse

until you are astride a corpse. Cling to it,

repeating your words to yourself.

Keep your mouth upon its mouth.

Stay engaged with the corpse in this manner,

until the critical moment arrives. At the critical moment,

you will feel the tongue of the corpse

protrude from between its lips. Continue

to exclude all other thoughts as failure

to control the body now will result

only in death. When you feel the tongue

fully between your teeth, bite down firmly,

cleaving through the muscle.

Once separated from its tongue,

the corpse will collapse. You may then

pull your mouths apart.

Return the corpse to the table.

Pass your hand across its eyes. Salt the tongue

before cleansing your hands, your mouth,

your own eyes. Sit to the left of the body,

hands resting upon it lightly, until sunrise.

At that point, thoughts may once again

be allowed to flood the mind. Words

used this night have been exhausted.

Let them go. Bow deeply upon taking your leave.

Handled this way, our journey together this evening should prove to be nothing but an honor.

I

Inside the whale, it is as if
you have always been inside a whale,
as if there is only inside the whale.
It is as if there was *before the whale*
and *now*. And in *now*
you will always be inside a whale.

Inside the whale, you do not understand
why you are inside a whale. It is even difficult
to determine it is a whale. You may recall
the sea, and the ship, and going over the side,
but the whale you never saw. (Q-What is
the hardest angle for identifying whales?
A-From inside the whale.)

From inside the whale, you cannot guide
the whale. A whale will do as a whale will do.
You may throw your body to one side
or another to try to steer the whale;
you may attempt to use the power
of your mind to influence the whale.
Your mind is of a greater capacity
than the whale's mind, but again,
a whale will do what a whale will do.

When inside the whale, it is best to be
inside the whale. Do what you are inside

the whale to do. Of course, you may use
only what was with you when thrown
overboard. No one packs to go inside
the whale. However, you should not try
to agitate the whale. It doesn't help
if the whale ejects you too far from shore.
Unfortunately, you have forgotten about *shore*
and think there is only *inside the whale*.

When you find yourself inside a whale,
meditate and practice journeys
to *outside the whale*. Know these
are skills that must be rehearsed
before needed. Hear the pitch
in his tenuous rumble, taste the acid
of his gentle lurp. Consider the feel
of baleen brushing against skin
and the way his rough tongue reopens
your atrophied, unremembered eyes.

Matt Talbot walked Dublin
with crushed glass in his socks.
With barbed wire around his chest.
Chains wrapped his right arm
and knee, cords on the other side.
Hid these bindings beneath his clothes.
Crossed the city's river moving from mass
to mass this way because he found himself
a slave to the Virgin.

Carried bricks for a living. Made alms
of what he earned. Slept only
on a plank. Kept but a timber
for his pillow. Never swore.
Took the pledge. No tobacco. Told no one
how he lived for pride in devotion
he thought the most devious sin of them all.

Bound his body to learn his body.
Learned his body to forget
his body. How else to get to empty.
How else to reach freedom but by journey.
Back and forth across the waters
beneath the monkey puzzle trees.
Walked quickly. Head down.
How else to approach her
but with a tested heart made toom.

A slave amn't I. My body a coffle
chained in one world
driven to the next. There's mornings
I think of heaving me
over the bridge. Nights I dream
I cross the river north
to hide myself from myself.
To keep me off my trail.

But there's no smarts in that.
This river runs a knife
that guts the city's middle.
These monkeys cross it daily
forever looking down.

Amn't I a slave to the Virgin.
Amn't I a hod-carrier for the Lord.

Britt understood what Parham meant
when he talked about Schrödinger's cat.
On rotation days, there's little but talking
and taking turns at the scope until
it's night or a sandstorm
and then it's walking and hoping lines
haven't shifted and the company
is where they were last.

Stick a cat in a box with something unstable,
a WMD, say. Until you lift the top to check, Britt,
that fucker is both alive and dead at the same time.
You know what that means?

It meant Schrödinger
had sat out the War to End All Wars
in Dublin, Clontarf actually,
escaping the Nazis twice
first Germany, then Austria
Ireland neutral, where they called it
The Emergency, Ré na Práinne in Irish
a dying language containing
neither a simple *yes* nor *no*
instead a *We will* or *We won't*
an *I am* or *I amn't*
neutrality a construct
continually fragile and balanced

on edge, like Clontarf, the coastal town
where Brian Boru ended the Irish-Viking Wars
although there were Irish and Vikings
on both sides, Munster against Leinster really
with Vikings serving according to their interests
and where Schrödinger grew blinder by the day.

WHAT

ELSE   What else should I want. But to

be a boy. A boy. At his mother's hip.

A boy between. His father

and the plow. A boy to remain.

What else.

When a boy. I ran fevers.

In these fevers. I ran circles.

Pursued. Front stairs up.

Back stairs down. No bright

lines. Only constant threshold.

How as a boy did I know. Some houses

had one stairs for family. One stairs

for help. During fevers

I knew not. If I was sick.

Or a betrayer of the other worlds.

As a boy. I thought picking up

the gun would make me. No longer

a boy. As a boy with a gun. I thought

being elsewhere. Made me

a different boy. As a boy with a gun

and a different tongue. I thought

returning home. Would bring me home.

What else did I. But run. What else

should I dream. But of home.

And home and home. What else to want.

But to be a boy and a boy and a boy.

dreamed I was a big tall man dreamed I drove
through Richmond never getting lost dreamed
I lay in the heat of Seven Sisters dreamed I was
the latest in the line of Byrds dreamed it was
the day of my recrudescence

dreamed I mapped the Great Dismal dreamed
Creeley surveyed while I mopped his eye
dreamed I made love to a younger sister
and made her in love with me while I intended
to get the older dreamed Hope
became a name for a boy

dreamed I was the first American suicide bomber
dreamed I buried Baby Charles Peter in the garden
and from his head grew beans dreamed I ate
those beans and gave birth to Baby Charles Peter

dreamed I did that thing you asked would I do
for you if you would do that thing for me
dreamed of our love's quiescence dreamed
my sins were many dreamed my sufferings few
dreamed I was one of the Lost Boys of Lee Marvin
dreamed I was a bastard son of Johnny Cash

DEAR ST.
GERTRUDE

—John Brown to
Gertrude Stein
December 1, 1859

I say *saint* because saint you are to me,
your one saintly eye the blazing sun, the other
a moon hung in the daytime sky. Folded
into bank of river, into elbow of tree, I watch you
watch me. It is the job of the sainted to see.

When on the run, I learned to sleep
with the barrel of the gun pointing
the direction I wished to resume travel.
But no vigilance is ever enough.
In the night, one voice whispers
Doddering Parent. The answer
Thankless Child.

St. Gertrude, come tonight for tomorrow
when I rise I swing and die on high
a man both crazed and right. As gallows
come to dot this nation, pray for us now
and in all times. When all of the people
are at fault, may all of the people be forgiven.
It is the job of the sainted to sort.

I come this evening a low man
crossing on knees to altar,
praying for intercession. As Americans
who write America, St. Gertrude,
we are astronauts made to practice

underwater as if it were space. Help the world
to see as we have seen.

St. Gertrude, write an America
that practices belief by believing,
that rehearses for space in space.
Make us believe as the mother believed.
Open the coffin lid. Let them see
what they did to a boy. His shoes filled
with gravel, he wears a corset of barbed wire.
The job of the sainted is simple.

Agitation is the work, St. Gertrude,
and yours are arms made to churn butter.
Point your muzzle towards America
and dream. Through this night and all others,
keep us in your sight.

I remain,

Yours St. Gertrude.
Sincerely, Devoutly, With Nary a Doubt,

John Honest to God Brown,
Writing From America, Underground.

John Brown, I want to write you a poem. I want to write
a big poem of America and I want to write it just for you.
I want to talk about the people and the place and sing them
just to you, so nobody else can hear. I want to do this
just for you, John Brown. I'm going to stay up tonight
and write America for nobody else but you.

I want to tell you about the Mormons and the Mexicans
and the Chinese. We all walked somewhere, John Brown,
and that is not just nostalgia. Everybody's been left one place
and told walk to another sometime. Don't die
while you're walking and that's when the poem
of America gets made.

That's the story of Mexicali, John Brown. Mexicali
got founded by Chinese, Chinese what lived
like cigarettes. A man wrote *When the tunnel
was set aflame, they streamed out just like ants.*
I never seen anything like that, John Brown,
and I doubt you did too.

A Mexican sea-captain put the first Chinese ashore
and told 'em *Walk to the hill. That hill
is where you want to be.* But it was miles and miles
to that hill, John Brown, and they died walking
through a desert. Them Chinese didn't know

from a desert, so they kept walking till they all
dropped and they weren't nowhere close to that hill yet.

And your Chinese carry memory a long time, John Brown.
Mexican sea captain learned that fact. Chinese
settled Mexicali hunted the Mexican sea captain down
with a vampire they grew in the ground. Except
it wasn't really a vampire, but a blind Chinese
with teeth grew up through his lip. But that
blind Chinese could always find the sea captain,
same way you always know if the man
bunks above is sleeping or awake. Being cellies,
John Brown, is how it was between that sea captain
and the vampire.

Those later Chinese bore that tale of walking
and dying. It's how the Chinese came to dig.
Dig to get under where it's cool. Dig to get under
where there's water. Digging's how the Chinese
found gold. Digging's how the Chinese built
the railroad I walk now. Chinese learned to get under,
telling that tale amongst themselves.

Telling tales is why the Chinese come to Mexicali
knew heat would kill 'em. And there wasn't nothing
there at the time, John Brown. No Mormons,

no Mexicans, no nobody wanted to live in that heat,
so wasn't nothing there at all. But the Chinese
just set to digging. First, they slept in a shallow,
then a hole. Them holes they made into cellars
and put stores and restaurants up top.
They connected all those cellars and lived
in the tunnels between to keep out the heat.
They lived in them tunnels stacked like cigarettes
in a box. They lived down there close like that
till the night of the fire.

Nobody living knows how that fire started,
John Brown. Some say enchilada man
dumped his coals the wrong place. Some say
it was spirits. Could be there comes a time
a Chinese vampire might sour on memory
and walking the earth. Them Mexicans and Mormons
didn't even know the Chinese was living down there
till they seen them all coming out the ground.

There was a whole Chinese city living up under
the earth, John Brown, and most people
didn't have the slightest. Won't you or I
ever see it at all. You think on that too much
and you couldn't never believe it. But why not
believe, John Brown. Why not believe it all.

This poem's the story of America, John Brown,
and I wrote it just for you. It's a big poem
of the story of America and I worked on it all night
to finish it for you. Your America is a big, long poem,
John Brown, and I wrote it all down tonight
so I could tell it, just to you.

Before Number 1 was gone. That's how soon
it began. How soon I began to dream.
Dream what the town could be like
with him in it. What my world
would be like with him in it.
How it would feel like Bible times.
Like long ago times. Times when giants
strode the earth.

By Number 16, he was already legend.
Not so much for the number he drank
but for the way he drank them. For how little
the bottle looked in his hand.
For how frustrated he grew
with the bottle's narrow neck.
Which is why I became the first
to speak. *You might want to try
a Mickey's. Those ones come in a widemouth.*

Number 32 and everybody's on talking terms
as he taught us things to say in French.
Abattage for Johnny Blue who came in
off shift from the chicken plant. *Un bourrique*
to Johnny Britt, who swore he'd whooped bigger
one night off base. *Et patati
et patata* when Britt wouldn't stop
his jawing, and after Britt hit him,

un plouc, as he pressed Britt over his head
and lobbed him out the door. We handed him
Number 53 and he was ours.
Our beautiful giant.
Like one man standing atop another.
Two men stapled side by side.

Number 76 found him spinning tales.
He drove me to school when I no longer
fit on the bus. 'Dede' he called me,
like the play he wrote.
It was theater, you see. With him,
it was all theater. 'A country road.
A tree. Evening.' and then
he gave what we came to know
as Lucky's speech *The skull*
the skull in Connemara
quaquaquaquaquaqua.

Ellerbe is a place where a man
feels appreciated he announced
before Number 94 and I swear
my heart swole with the promise
when he and Johnny Locklear
shook on a price for the farm
over Number 109. *No gift is bestowed*
but the Lord has done it Locklear prayed.

We thank you for the mighty weapon
you have delivered upon this town tonight.

Number 156 and we'd run out of beer
and though this could have turned our giant,
he stayed. Though he could have
wreaked vengeance and destroyed us all
with a flick, with a blow, with his rage,
he didn't, he never did. He merely
laid down his head and slept. And that spot
was his for years until he died there
a few months back. *Blood probably wore out*
it had to travel so far. One hell of a trip
the length of him was Britt's theory.

When little girls in this town
jump rope they sing
A pot of tea
A spotted dog
One-five-six
and the giant falls
quaquaquaquaqua.

The People's Act of Love requires courage every day.
The People's Act of Love requires silence, requires listening.
The People's Act of Love requires more from the people
than the people think they have to offer,
more than the people believe they can deliver.

Chairman Mao Inspects Areas North and South
of the Yangtze River. Chairman Mao Instills
Courage in the People. Chairman Mao Looks Over
the People's Act of Love. Chairman Mao Turns to Dust.

The People's Act of Love is for the people.
The People's Act of Love never has enough people.
The people ask for more from The People's Act of Love
but The People's Act of Love is exhausted, frankly,
if you don't mind The People's Act of Love being frank.

And sometimes, The People's Act of Love grows tired
of the people, of the act of love. It would be nice
to have a Saturday night in. A good curry.
Maybe a movie. Curl up on the couch.
The People's Act of Love wonders
if these are the right things to ask of the people.

Chairman Mao Promises Two Goats
for Every Family. Chairman Mao Delivers
the People's Goats. The People's Goats Graze

in Areas North and South of the Yangtze River.
Chairman Mao Inspects the People's Grazing Goats.

The goats also turned against The People's Act of Love.
Really, it just got to be too much, all that fuss,
all that time. And the People's Act of Love always believed
in itself a little more than it should have probably.
You can see it in any of the pictures.
(The People's Act of Love could also stand
to lose that stupid hat.) And some days,
The People's Act of Love smells a little too much
like patchouli. Though it is hard to say such things
to The People's Act of Love. The People's Act of Love
can be sensitive sometimes.

The People's Act of Love stands in line at Mao's Tomb.
The People's Act of Love harvests the dust
blossoming atop the tomb before it exits
The Gates of Beauty, returning home to release
its goats to graze on the north bank of the Yangtze.
The People's Act of Love renews its courage
and rededicates itself to silence, to listening.
Such are the days of The People's Act of Love.

AIN'T I
PRETTY

Muhammad Ali been noticing lately
an increase in animals rising up. An increase
in animals acting like they are fed up
with being et up. Animals acting like
people in the way and the time has come
for us to move. Porpoises raping people.
A stingray stick his tail straight in the heart
of a man petting him. Chimpanzee
rip his neighbor lady's face off her head.
Like the food chain unlinking itself
to join up some different way again.

Mountain lion eat a jogger. Antelope
wipe out a boy on a bike. A whole rash
of feral chickens roaming New Orleans
and I bet every last one of them
is getting tired of being fried.

Noticing is what Ali's tasked to do now
and ain't I pretty while I do it. Man so pretty
ought not to be locked up so tight.
But sitting so pretty, staying so still
always been the way I fight. Fall back
against the ropes and let the world
punch itself out. It lean in close
and you taunt it awhile *Done told you*

it takes two men to whup me
and you ain't but one.

Alligator bite a police car. Giant rats
eating cheeks off babies. Kangaroos
rampage, bees gone killer.
Elephants trample a whole village
but we still teaching dolphins
how to bomb a submarine.

These are shifting times and nobody
appreciate the man who say so.
But Ali done stared up
what knocked me down.
Ali the one made to see
cause I already know what it feel like
when old bottom rail slide up top.

How many men walk the docks. How many stop
to consider panthera tigris tigris. How many fail
to see tiger. How hard not to mimic tiger's growl,
tiger's swat. How hard to see tiger chained
and not think *Me Mine It*. How small is the cage
of possession. How hard it is not to buy a tiger.

How hard it is to be the tiger. How do pug marks
circle. How intent is tiger on leaving. How weak
are the bonds of man. How far into swamp
does tiger go. How does man chase believing
this is who he is. The Man Who Owns Tiger.
Believing in man. Believing in tiger.

How tree forms shapes for tiger. How tiger takes shape
under tree. How tiger chuffs to tree. How swamp gas
beckons man. How man feels he is called. (*Deeper in.*
Deeper in.) How the chase turns his mind to himself.
How night deludes. How future retreats.
How man last knows this life. As man. As tiger.

How thick pulls root. How tangled swims bladderwort.
How swallowed can man be. How the story of were-tiger
grows. How children play this out. How they contest
to see who will be tiger. By hands shaped into claw of tiger.
With a lunge and the growl of tiger. Between the stripes
of tiger. How hard it is not to be the tiger.

LADY WONDER

When Lady Wonder, the Mind–Reading Horse
tested *Telepathic* the first session
but *Inconclusive* the next,
Dr. Rhine naturally concluded
that Lady's abilities had departed
stealthily, like they had arrived.

After all, Lady had not only matched
Circle, Cross, Square, and Star
accurately, she could at her horse typewriter,
nose out answers to any question read aloud.
Mesopotamia Carolina Hindustan
Lady composed block by block
after the student whispered
Where Will I Find Riches? Love? Die?

When not dealing with the public,
Lady liked to listen to the radio,
especially when Big John dialed in WDIA
as he mucked out the stall. *Horse
raised on the bottle away from other horses
don't know if it a horse, a chicken, or a people*
he explained to Little John
while Ruth Brown sang *Done stood it
till I can't stand it no more* and Lady
paced and nodded along in the paddock.

Ignorance of your own kind
require a Memphis blues.

From the radio is where Lady first learned
of the missing children. As soon as she heard
the news, she began to flip blocks
and spelled out *Pittsfield Water Wheel.*
When the body was found
near the Field and Water Pit, the police
brought her cases in droves.

At Lady's final séance, the weeping mother
pleaded *What has happened*
to my babies? What's become
of my Claudia, my Hans?
Lady nuzzled the typewriter to explain
that the children were already dead
and would be found together
on a Sunday, under the water, near a tree.
And that was the end. Lady
never spoke again.

When Dr. Rhine returned for the second round
of tests—cards, questions, basic math—
Lady simply refused. *Telepathy*
comes and goes Rhine reassured his class.

That horse has been right about everything
except what day those German children
would be found.

Lady rubs her rump against a tree,
then gums the apple off the ground.
She wonders of warning the tups and ewes
humans think their grief unique
and the world is mostly water.

At first, it is unimaginable. That God would choose you.
That you would be chosen by God. That God has something
that is only for you. That something exists that is only
between you and God. That God would send a whale.
That a whale could hunt you down. That you would be swallowed
by a whale. That you can live in the belly of a whale.

In the belly of a whale, the pressure changes when the whale
dives or breeches. You feel that change in pressure and think
I am in the belly of a whale. I am on a mission from God
just as this whale is on a mission from God. But there comes
a point. The whale completes his mission
and he spits you out. God's plan concludes
and he spits you out. The whale and God
go missing. The whale and God
no longer come around.

So you decide to look and you begin to notice.
The crow who flies figure eights above your head.
The birds who whistle your name in a kind of harmony.
The tiger who paces the cage with eyes only for you.
The pile of wolf scat left under the tree outside your window.
The way the wind quickens when you step though a door.
And you think *Yes, God. Yes.*
I am ready. I feel the change in pressure.
This time I can be but humble. This time
I will say only yes.

And you think of your time inside the whale.

How inside the whale you knew where you were.

How inside the whale you could focus only on being

inside a whale. How you can feel the size

of the whale from inside the whale. How it is

to be a tiny man inside a giant whale.

How there is no God but God inside any whale.

So you begin to tell the story of your time

inside the whale, first to friends, then for pay.

How each night you scan the audience

sure the whale will show, sure that God

will show. How you are looking

while you are talking. How during your talking,

the people nod but you know what they are really thinking.

They are really thinking *He acts as if he did something,*

living inside a whale. But it was God.

God did something, keeping him alive

inside that whale. And the whale.

The whale did something, being a messenger of God.

But him. He just rode along, silent, and wept.

As if to weep were nothing.

As if riding were a passive act.

As if silence isn't a practice of faith.

Then, at the end of the night, the pressure

shifts again and they come to shake your hand

and they say *Yes. Your words. Now I know.*
After all the talking and after shaking
all the hands, the night ends and you are left
with little except that God and the whale
were not here again. There is all the talking
and there is all the shaking but the night
comes to its end and you think only *No.*
No one knows. No one knows my words,
except for the whale and God and me.

II

BOYISHLY

the summer that summer. the summer
I was prevented. each morning
that summer my eyes matted shut.
sleep my mother called what joined them.
warm water and a washcloth before
I could see. so much water that summer
and then the sun. that summer the fruit
ripened rapidly. the drone

that summer. a boyish summer. the summer
I took the boyish waters. like being
drowned that summer. that summer I practiced
pulling my t-shirt on like a boy (2 arms
neck) not a girl (neck 2 arms). that summer
my mother warned *You're getting too big*
to jump down the stairs like that. all summer
I wore orange plaid toughskins
and my *show me state* shirt. each day
that summer I ate french toast for breakfast.
every noon that summer, a hot dog for lunch.
that summer I knocked myself out
jumping down the stairs and woke thinking
She cannot find me

here like this. that summer I watched
our great dane get opened up
by a bean truck. *I never even saw her*

mourned the driver *then*
she was just there. the summer
my already dead grandmother came to visit
only me. I saw a wolf lope through the corn
each dusk that summer. that summer
I threw rocks to make murders of crows

rise from the field, the summer I fell
in love with their flocking fell in love
with their love. after rain that summer
tiger shadows gathered in the waterway.
everything circled that summer
everything promising
you may come join us

whenever you like. that summer I read folded
in the apple tree. that whole summer
watched on high. all that sun that summer
and then the rain. the fruit ripened rapidly.
it seemed the summer that summer
was never done.

CROSS

OVER   The hardest part of learning to cross the street
               is the both/and, looking both left and right,
               thinking as both pedestrian and driver, being
               always already both here
               and on the other side.

               At the end of the driveway, my father
               and I sometimes go left. From there
               we cross the busy street
               to the White Hen Pantry
               where he buys me a Pepsi.
               By the time we return home, I will be
               crunching ice despite
               his warnings not to.

               Other nights we walk
               straight down the drive
               and across to the park
               where he teaches me to golf
               on the edge of the public course,
               the 14th hole facing my window.
               Each night, I fall
               asleep watching my ghost
               chip out of sand traps.

               On either trip, he makes me
               walk him home, holding his hand

and deciding when it is safe to cross.

Left and right and left again
I mouth at the corners
but still cannot get it correct,
pulled back on the curb for overlooking
the truck that is turning,
the bicyclists, legs churning,
heads down. For imaging us
safely on the other side
before it is clear, our time.

TAKE,

SAVE,   My mother likes to go for groceries alone

GO   but my dad is restoring an auto

        and would like to be left on his own

so this Saturday we tag along.

        My sister is only a few months old and is sleeping

still when we return, but I am

        big enough to recall a street full

of screaming fire engines and ambulances.

        In the other world of night, when I get up to help

with my sister, (a promise made

        upon the announcement of her arrival)

my mother says she knew to bring

        the baby yesterday because a voice had told her so.

Something soft, whispered,

        leaving an imprint of *take, save, go.*

        Cross with impatience, my father

had been inside at the kitchen

        table instead of changing the oil

on the street, when a woman

        weaved through the trees in the park,

cut catty-corner full speed ahead,

        destroyed the jeep, and jumped the curb

into our house. The front of the car came to rest

        on my sister's crib and the woman's purse

ended up on my bed. She had been dead

before she entered the golf course

and only in the morning's paper

    does my mother learn

this woman was her mother's neighbor

    who had driven 75 miles

to suffer a stroke, but weave safely

    through a labyrinth of trees,

to discover her next door

    neighbor's grandchild's crib

at the heart of the maze. A day

    that began with coffee and country

on the radio came to a halt on a

    floor, voices shouting aloud to stay

on the edges, crossing the middle

    only finds you the Minotaur,

half-man, half-bull, kept in the center

    by his father in shame and fury, who,

it turns out, is someone you

    almost knew.

CHILD OF
WOLVES

I think I am special my sister confesses at 5.
The ghosts told Mom to bring me or else
I would have died when the car drove
right into the house right into our room
right into my bed. As her older sister
I am once again forced to remind her
that she is already special because she
is the child of wolves left at our doorstep
to raise. That we had been forced to shave her
so others might believe her human –
no person baby would naturally be that bald.
That her wolf parents had named her
Yipping Girl Prowl. That some nights still
she awakens me with a howl
calling for the home she neither
fully forgets nor remembers.
(It is to be both captured and freed
to be raised among another species.)
Maybe we are both wolf babies she hopes
and fears, but I disclose I can only
trust the story the parents tell me
for I have no way to know
no older sister to witness my coming
to tell me the truth of my birth.
She speculates *I bet you had a sister when you arrived*
but late one night she aggravated you

and in a fit you later forgot, you ate her.
Still she says *I think that I am special.*

**THE
RUPTURES
OF THIS
WORLD.
THIS
WORLD
WITH
ALL ITS
DAYS.**

Imagine this. All morning, Mary, the youngest,
on the cusp of it all (it all), mute, long stare
as if a trance. Returning from church,
she speaks again. Says *I don't know you.*
Says *Don't call me Mary. My name is Rita.*
Says *Take me back. My family. I miss them.*
Says *Now.* Says *Please.*

Adolescents, already so absent.
Always spinning. Hoping to whirl away.
Not yet realizing. There's so few places to go.
That most come back sooner. Maybe later.
Daughters the worst for this desiring.
For this space.

As one who loves, there's nothing but to listen.
Despite having heard the body of Rita L–
was found this morning. Snuck away
to meet a boy in the night.
Perhaps eloping. Girl children
always escaping. Attempting.
(Imagine if such release can be borne.)

Knock on the door. Not even getting out
*My daughter awakened believing
she is yours* before the girl has thrown herself
into the other's arms. Cries *Mother.*

Recognizes everyone. Knows where
the teapot is kept. Which canister
holds the leaves. Gives Mrs. L–
two lumps in hers. Asks
if you prefer lemon or cream.
Despite having made your tea
since she was eight. Despite never having seen
a lemon. This world run over with such ruptures
when we can bear to look.

What else then to consider.
Too cruel not to leave her behind
yet all the way home *That was not
Mary's body at the bottom of that hole,
well cover rotten above.* But never a question.
Never how. Never why.

Presenting this story to students
I say *a different time.* Provide explanations.
Like *epilepsy.* Like *morphine, opium.* Like *hysteria.*
Use time to create space. Still, all things
potentially spongy. No vigilance ever enough.
Later, I read *Down in the hole, lingeringly,
the gravedigger puts on the forceps*
then sleep the whole night through.
Imagine that.

Another day. Footsteps on the porch.

A knock against the door.

On the other side, Mary.

Her body now pushing breasts.

Says *Mother* again, then tears.

Mrs. L– also weeping. Having wept

the entire way. *She's done I think.*

Gone. Vanished once more.

(Imagine losing the same one twice.)

Girl children the worst of all.

For space. For desire. For living in this world.

This world with all its days.

ROSE
GOES TO
SUNDAY
SCHOOL
IN THE
NEW
WORLD

When I take the broken down boxes
to the trash in the back, I meet
the daughter, Rose, first.
You are not the person who lives there
she begins over our shared fence.
Rose is just a child, settled and warm,
and I am unsure how to warn her
that I desire a home and have moved here
solely with the goal of living somewhere
for more than 10 months.
So I may cease being the wandering academic.
So I can begin to imagine a new, still life.
So I might unpack books and actually leave them
one place long enough, they would
one day be layered in dust.

When we meet in the backyard,
Rose has a question for me.
Are you a girl or a boy she wants to know.
She pauses when I ask her which she thinks I am
and says *It's hard to tell. You have boy hair*
but a girl voice. Paired together
in me like this, she's unsure what to value
more and continues her interrogation.
What's your favorite thing in the sky
she asks. *Birds* I say and learn
that girls should say rainbows.

What's the best thing in the sea
she quizzes. *I'm not sure* I confess.
Mermaids, I guess. She nods, close enough.
Boys, she says, *will always answer shark.*

At 6, Rose is still unconvinced, but one
of her mothers reads me better, offering
My partner and I live here with Rose, our daughter.
Come over and visit whenever.
It's always nice to have family near.

I next see Rose at the neighborhood grocery.
You live next door to me she announces.
I agree and tell her how much I like her new jungle gym.
It is a large wooden boat, nearly 12 feet tall, which
fills her backyard. The stern is open at the bottom
to get to a sandbox inside,
there is a ladder to climb to the upper deck,
plenty of rope rigging for scaling the sides,
and a slide for abandoning ship in a hurry.
She says it's an ark and tells me of Sunday school
and how they learned you measure arks in cubits
not in feet. How two of every animal
as well as Noah's family could fit inside his together.
How when the bird comes back it means
it's time to get out on to a world that is safe,
washed clean. How her mommies won't let her

play on hers until they make
the soft place to land underneath.

Three days later, when the mulch is in place,
I return from work to an ark
full of Asian girls. Rose's playgroup
of adopted Chinese daughters
is inaugurating the space, and it is almost
as if those girls have sailed here together
to choose the parents that wait for them
safely, inside, on dry land
and I wonder how these girls
will come to discuss this voyage in the future,
as Middle Passage or Kindertransport.

Today though, Rose spots me and I am introduced.
This is Tanya. She has boy hair, but she's a girl too.
Immediately there are protests
She's not wearing any makeup.
She has on boy shoes.
I tell them in my best girl voice that I really
do not like sharks and they are convinced.
Get in the boat they scream together.
You're standing in the middle of the water.

On the upper deck of the ark
we take tea together, talk of school

and teachers, consider the many beauties
of both sea and sky, swap tips
for safe transit, and wait for the
sign of the dove, so we will know
that not only will the rains have stopped
but the waters will have receded
and it will be time to get out, to disembark
onto a world where the ground
is both loose enough so it may take
new roots and dry enough so that dust
may finally begin to layer itself
into beautiful blossoms.

THE

SACCADES

Imagine bring Dracula or Van Helsing. People insist
on fictional, yet bodies bear witness
all around. There are were-foxes, crows,
whales and tigers, but we speak only
of the wolf. Reinhold Messner discovers
footprints of Yetis, then spends a whole book
dithering over whether they are from the grey species
or the red. Oh how I tire of circles. Let there be
horizontal. Let there be vertical. Let us move across instead.

Remote viewing experts employed by a military
of the future call in to the overnight show
and agree on the challenges in explaining the future
to the past. They insist we do not see them around us
because we do not expect to. (These types of moments
are called predictive saccades.) *Yes* they answer
the caller. *The things of your pockets*
travel with you across time. Now we know
that was not the question to ask.
What is our nostalgia for drowning?
Who among us will notice the ruptures first?
When do we cease to waste the talents of the dead?
These are the questions, when given a chance,
we should have asked of the future.

And this era is the end of our Olsons.
We have cycled the line out. Micro-saccades

are continual and we see because we fill in
what we trust we will find. The woman across the street
sometimes believes I am me, sometimes believes
I am my husband. She nods when I tell her
I have no husband. *Good. Never marry them.*
Makes them lazy. The impossibility
of verbal corrections to visual errors.
The occular tremor. The occular drift.

Maybe the floaters in my vision are nano-UFOs
from the future. Maybe this is the way
we eventually go across time. Maybe inside
my non-existent husband and child sleep curled.
Saccades can become guided by memory
and I learn to recognize my husband Augustus
and our little Nathaniel, one lanky and taciturn,
the other, blue-eyed from the Swedish
lying hidden inside me. They are my wolf and crow
circling the house each night. They are
two black boxes pinging at the bottom of the sea.

HOW I REMEMBER DRINKING

those mornings a steady knocking.
my head on the shower wall.

evening's lapses became palpable.
the core of these lapses dense.
dense like the heart of the sun.
lapses of a palpable density.
a weight at the hub of it all.
no thread to follow from the core.

those mornings, a memory of heat.
heat like the core of the sun.
my head recalls the heart of the sun.
shower walls palpable.
wings lost again.
too near the sun. too near the sea.

in the shower, words drown
in their own density. denial is sewn
into the hub of my words.
mistakes hold together with wax and with thread.

morning lapses turn more daedalus than icarus.
one drowned while cleaving the sky.
the other held in a labyrinth of his own devise.
those mornings more labyrinth than maze.

no path to follow no opening to find.

only mornings of steady knockings.
my head on the shower wall.

THE
OLD OLD
OLD OLD
VERY OLD
WOMAN

At first, I thought the walkers

might be the army men I watch float

down from the sky. But the army men

fall from the sky with direction

and purpose and this is not

how the walkers walk. When they walk

the walkers do not carry anything

with them though sometimes

they push a bike and I wonder

what the walkers are walking to

or where the walkers are walking from

and why the walkers do not ride

the bikes they push for this road

runs from one turnoff to nowhere

to another turnoff to nowhere and

in between the nowhere there is nothing

but swamp and field and loblollys and me.

I also know the army men cannot

be the walkers for the army men never

land on the road itself. Instead

the army men drift behind the pines

into what I imagine must be a field

that once was full of tobacco

or cotton or cantaloupes and now

has been softened and prepared

for only the army men to land upon.
I think they have made this field
so dry and fluffy for the army men
a smoke of dust must rise
when each army boot strikes the ground.

But still I think one day
the army men will walk this road
and unlike the walkers
the army men will not be afraid
of a woman who lives in a ditch
and so when I call to them
they will come to me
even if it is the dark part
of morning even if it
is a moonless night and they
will call me *ma'am* and they
will use their army strength
to lift me from the ditch
and the first thing I will say
after *Thank You!* is *Do you have*
a cigarette for I would kill
for a cigarette and of course
one of them will for they
are army men and army men
love to smoke.

After army men my favorite thing

to watch adrift in the sky

are the sharp-shinned hawks

bombing the chinquapins

eating while on wing. I love

to pretend I am the one soaring

and I practice using my raptor eyes

to spy on that woman

who lives on her back in the ditch

near the swamp and in my hawk mind

I think *She looks as if she could use*

a present a cigarette maybe

although I know hawks

would more likely bring a junebug

to walk the hills of my knuckles

or a grasshopper who would spit

tobacco juice in my eye

to make me release him

and I would be grateful to any hawk

that brought me those fine presents as well.

I believe in the army men for one evening

I watched a walker toe a yellowbelly slider

onto his back in the middle of the road

and that turtle just pulled his legs

out of the air and into his shell

and though I do not know

how it happened by the next morning

he had righted himself and was gone

and though I have missed him ever since

I like to think that after his trek

from one side of the road

to the other that turtle slid

into the swamp at dawn and told

the other rising turtles of all he had seen

the walkers and the army men

and of cigarettes and about the woman

in the ditch whose legs stayed stuck up

and how she had junebugs and grasshoppers

for friends and how everything in the world of the road

the air the sun the dirt was hard

and how you only had to make one mistake

and if you were lucky you would live to regret it

how it took luck and timing

and fortitude but you could still

live long enough to regret it

the one mistake you made out there

on that long straight road

III

More of the woman, shifting her hips, moving through birds.
More of the birds rising together, fashioning a flock.
More of the birds, reporting to crow, reporting on woman.
More flying together to bring crow the tale of woman
and her love of the bird, the flocking of birds their fashion of love.
More of their quickening. More of her hips. More of the shift.

More of the crow tracking the woman, tracing her movement
through copse and through fen. More surveying heat, more
hastening blood. More of the clouds talking of crow, listening
to crow. Crow's wing at the hair of the woman. Crow's beak
in the ear of the woman. More of the clouds climbing down
mountains. More of the listening. More of the telling.

More of the trees singing to birds. More of the birds
called to the trees. More birds in tree elbows, cradled
in the elbows of trees. More talk of the woman who makes
heads of crows, who dons the head of a crow. More of her
love for crow. Climbs the tree, shifts her hips, rousts the birds.
More of the shift. More of her hips. More of the quick of birds.

You can die with a giant wad of love
jammed up in your heart, your heart
a mine shaft stuffed full of sub-bituminous coal
no one thinks worth taking. Everyone else
can find a miner to scuttle out their veins.
Everyone else has a miner who shows up for work daily
and chops and blasts and digs and hauls
and there is runoff and poisoned water occasionally,
but that is just the cost of change in America.
Decapitated mountains are the price
we are willing to pay for love in America.
But no one, no one has ever been
adversely affected by a shaft collapse
or pitching seams in my heart. No one has died
or become trapped there. There is no need
to send down a canary because I am green.
My love is green, America. My love is sustainable.
It burns clean. It has its own czar
and a series of commercials urging you to adopt it
as a lifestyle. It has a marketing team
constructing eye-catching symbols
you too can attach to your packaging
to make you more attractive because
whether they ever act on it or not, when asked,
American consumers express an interest
in purchasing green products. But a sad, true fact
is they may be lying. They may only be stating

what they wish could be true, imagining a person

they wish they could be—an American who consumes

green products—but in real life, they may not be bothered

to keep a bin or compost or recycle.

And here is one other sad, true, ecological fact.

Some things of the earth remain in the earth.

They live and die in the earth. Some things of the earth

just lie in the earth, hardening, unrecognized,

and those things of the earth know that only inches

keep them from experiences like *bird* and *soft* and *weather*.

Those things of the earth just lie in the earth

hoping one day they will be something other

than of the earth. But a sad, true, ecological fact is

you can die having never left a grave of earth.

The sad, true, ecological fact is if you die

from your heart being jammed full of love

your heart will still be making more love

right up to the second you die. It is just a fact.

You can die with a giant wad of love jamming up your heart.

Everyone says Does she not know

Can she not tell Everyone says

She must know How could she not

know Everyone says It's so obvious

Even she must know Someone says Maybe

no one's ever said it to her Maybe no one

has ever told her Maybe she doesn't

know Everyone says She has to know

Someone says If a retarded kid

wants to be an astronaut no one says

Kid you're way too retarded to ever

be an astronaut No one says You can't even

name the planets No one says You don't know

how to count to ten Everyone says That's great

Work hard Keep trying Do your best

Someone says Surely she must know

Someone says Maybe she doesn't

know Maybe she can't tell Maybe

she thinks she can Maybe she thinks

she's capable Everyone gives her a hug

Everyone says You'll find the right one

someday Everyone says You know

it's not you Everyone says Keep your heart

open Everyone says The right one is out there

somewhere Everyone says Does she really not

know Surely she has to know Everyone knows

Someone says The moon is huge tonight

Someone says We'll all live there someday

Everyone says Maybe someone should just

tell her Someone says You would think

she would already know

There are gullywashers in Memphis
and in an upstairs window of Graceland,
she is facing the Meditation Garden
as if listening to a distant music,
when Lisa Marie finally turns to me
and says *Sweetie, if you can't get on board*
with Scientology, this thing between us,
it's through.

Later, that night, we are lying
yin-yang, head to toe,
in the king-sized bed when
I remind her it wasn't what we thought
that brought us together in that NASCAR bar.
She had liked me and my hair like her daddy's
the front with a curl, the back closely shorn.
That I had played Thin Lizzy's *Rosalie*
on the jukebox. You see, she always
dates the danger boy, just this time a different form.

I protest I cannot comprehend a world
created by hydrogen bombs, volcanoes,
and Xenu. She insists *Darlin', I believe in you.*
You must learn to suspend your disbelief
and trust me until all the facts are in.
I say *Baby, I am sleeping with a straight girl*

who was once married to Michael Jackson.
There is little left but trust in this world.

She curls into me, her head on my breast.
She ruffles the short hairs of my neck
and to the rhythm of the river shuffling off the eaves
sings *She knows music, I know music too you see.*
For that evening, while gently lifting the Mississippi
and quietly uniting the quick and the dead
rain was general all over Memphis.

OH

LEMUEL Captain Coffin promised

the barrel's contents was ours

if those boys landed *as healthy in Halifax*

as when they left old Siam.

That firkin of rum

floated through every boatswain's dream,

so we were nothing but smiles

when we swapped the salt horse in our meals

for the hardtack in theirs

and heated seawater to swab out their bunks.

Anything for you, Chang-Eng, Anything at all.

So the joined boys never knew our ship

as we did—a foul container afloat. Rats

bobbing in the water butt, duff as much

mealy worm as flour, or fleas and lice

so gorged and content

they couldn't be bothered

to jump from one man to the next.

Keeping alive amidst filth and deception

was tricks I learned at war. Our sergeant

didn't task us much with the

left flank, right flank, march

but deemed his job more the thinking kind.

Any people who seek to rent asunder

what the Good Lord chose to weave

are fools. It's the United States is, boys,
not the United States are.

That kind of soldiering
found me Danville Prison by fall,
gangrenous and driven though.
I is shot I fevered and mumbled for days
Shot, oh yes I are till Lemuel
stole apple cores from the hog's trough
and made a potmash to spread
atop my wounds. The winter
found us tarpmates and until
liberation that spring, I knew
as long as Lemuel was alive
I could be too. Paired, I come to think,
is how the Lord keeps us whole.

So the shavetails may have been bamboozled,
but I understood why that barrel rode along.
Locked in blood as they was,
if Chang passed away one evening,
Eng would be dead by dawn
and Captain Coffin would no more
throw that corpse over
than he would pitch a bag of coins
into a bawdy house, gone and then gone,
with nothing left to hold.

Alive, them boys was gold bars
but dead and preserved
they still could sell a ticket.

Healthy we delivered them though,
and the Oh Be Joyful flowed all night.
Many a man lost or won or gave away
his whole sail's pay but the sergeant
had taught us *A sober man*
should hide his greenbacks from any sot
but especially when the soaker is himself
so I set back to sea
with a sore head but full pockets.

A sailor when I mustered out
and it's asea I since remained
just as I imagine Lemuel
long stayed himself to land. Barber
maybe or mason, some crafted work
for his hands. I still can remember
the hot of the poultice when first he laid it on,
just as I remember the terrible punishment
in his tearing it off cool.
The Lord's vengeance
he lamented with me
often follows his grace.

This world is only a little ours
and I hope when those boys is buried
they lie them in the bone orchard
the way they lived above.
Death is no place to seek promise,
Lemuel Jeanpierre. I recall that
from our war as well. But today,
as my time falls upon me,
I find I cannot cry against it.

In death as in life.
Oh Lemuel.
I wish that wish for us all.

ABSOLUTELY A PARTICLE, ABSOLUTELY A WAVE

It is so cold outside, our discussion creates its own fog.
We are always standing on street corners talking,
before readings, amongst smokers at art openings,
after the party where we met, friends of friends. The circles
we run in strangely overlap. Driving all this talk is the principle
that enough blather keeps action at bay, but desire alive and at war.

The night of the party I hold forth (*Iran is already the next war.*
Iraq is forgotten and Afghanistan is quickly slipping into a fog.
Terrorism has been reduced from a human act to a mere principle.)
until you stop me, noting that simply the action of talking
theory abstractly recreates the same circles
I was criticizing. Perhaps if I'd had a better opening.

By now though, I am used to being challenged by you, the opening
up you demand, no hiding behind intellect, no matter how rattling the war
it introduces between head and heart, me and you. We circle
the path around the reservoir once more and your glasses fog
over when we duck inside the bar. Asked for orders, we stop talking
and glance at the clock. It is only 3pm, but I order two beers on the principal

belief that getting drunk is our only hope of moving beyond the principle
of indeterminacy in which we are stuck. It is your heart that needs opening
and your head shutting down. If you could just stop talking
about how you can't be in love with a woman, defuse that artificial war,

and stop seeing us the way others see us. (*Looking creates the very fog*
which disguises the observed.) Then I believe we could stop moving in circles

and step forward. Enough beer and we too could be dancing slow circles
in this bar. But, I also know the bartender would throw us out on principle,
(*No dykes dancing. It upsets the customers.*) and through the morning fog
of your hangover, you would already be distant, shutting down openings
created the night before, a perfect case of winning the battle but losing the war.
So instead, after the first pint, we leave and return to walking and talking.

It makes my head spin but leaves me strangely satisfied, all this talking, talking
as if talking were our way of doing, the way Heisenberg's atoms spun in circles
but never came together as a bomb. (*Did he really try or secretly sabotage the war?*)
Not everything worth pursuing is worth winning; losing is also an honorable principle.
We argue about this, hiding behind a smokescreen of words. At the opening
of the bar door, boys spill forth in squadrons and advance through the fog,

and we are still standing there talking, making mushroom clouds of fog.
This will continue until nothing changes. There are no openings in perfect circles.
It is bittersweet to live by principle; I wonder what it feels like to be victorious in war?

NOTES & ACKNOWLEDGMENTS

"Exclude All Other Thoughts" is based on *The Corpse Who Dances* from Alexandra David Neel's *Magic and Mystery in Tibet*.

"Eight Masculine Dreams of Charles Olson" contains a line from *William Byrd of Virgina: The London Diary* (1717-1721).

"A Poem For Old John Brown" is based on a story reported in William Vollmann's *Empire*.

First thanks go to Justin Boening. He is living proof a fine poet makes a fine editor. His eye and ear have been great friends to this book. Thanks as well go to KMA Sullivan. Her care for and generosity towards artists, poets in particular, is heroic in this day and age. Their love of *Boyishly* is priceless to me; thanks will never be enough.

Next, I owe a huge thank you to the Black Socks poetry group. They have been making me a better poet for eight years now. Special thanks go to Andrea Selch for showing me poetry from the publishing side as well. A crucial group of friends has heard and read these poems over the years. Their support makes this book and so much more possible.

This book is dedicated to my sister and nephew. Together, they have introduced me to a new level of family; it has been my great joy to have known and loved them each for every day of their lives. Special love goes as well to my dad and mom who made room for and encouraged books in my life from the beginning. My mother especially would have loved this book, although she would have hated its title.

Finally, thanks and more go to Susan Pietrzyk. Her presence in my life is reflected any place this book dares to imagine what it might feel like to be loved.

Some of these poems previously appeared in *Boston Review*, *Southword*, *PANK* online, *Fanzine*, *Pedestal*, *Main Street Rag*, *Redheaded Stepchild*, and *Cairn*. Thanks go to the editors and magazines for giving them their first home.

TANYA OLSON lives in Durham, North Carolina and teaches at Vance-Granville Community College. In 2010, she won the Discovery/*Boston Review* Prize and was named a 2011 Emerging Voices Fellow by the Lambda Literary Foundation.

ALSO FROM YESYES BOOKS

FULL-LENGTH COLLECTIONS

Heavy Petting by Gregory Sherl

Panic Attack, USA by Nate Slawson

I Don't Mind If You're Feeling Alone by Thomas Patrick Levy

The Youngest Butcher in Illinois by Robert Ostrom

If I Should Say I Have Hope by Lynn Melnick

Man vs Sky by Corey Zeller

Frequencies: A Chapbook and Music Anthology, Volume I

[SPEAKING AMERICAN BY BOB HICOK, LOST JULY BY MOLLY GAUDRY, AND

BURN BY PHILLIP B. WILLIAMS PLUS DOWNLOADABLE MUSIC FILES

FROM SHARON VAN ETTEN, HERE WE GO MAGIC, AND OUTLANDS]

VINYL 45s

A PRINT CHAPBOOK SERIES

Please Don't Leave Me Scarlett Johansson by Thomas Patrick Levy

Pepper Girl by Jonterri Gadson

POETRY SHOTS

A DIGITAL CHAPBOOK SERIES

Nocturne Trio by Metta Sáma

[ART BY MIHRET DAWIT]

Toward What Is Awful by Dana Guthrie Martin

[ART BY GHANGBIN KIM]

How to Survive a Hotel Fire by Angela Veronica Wong

[ART BY MEGAN LAUREL]

The Blue Teratorn by Dorothea Lasky

[ART BY KAORI MITSUSHIMA]

My Hologram Chamber Is Surrounded by Miles of Snow by Ben Mirov

[IMAGES BY ERIC AMLING]